Sign Language

ABC

Special thanks to Alli, my editor, for continued support.
And of course, to my three boys—I, E, and O—I love you.
— L. F. H.

STERLING CHILDREN'S BOOKS
New York

An Imprint of Sterling Publishing
387 Park Avenue South
New York, NY 10016

Lot#:
2 4 6 8 10 9 7 5 3 1
10/11

Sterling ISBN 978-1-4027-6392-2

For information about custom editions, special sales, premium and
corporate purchases, please contact Sterling Special Sales
Department at 800-805-5489 or specialsales@sterlingpublishing.com.

Designed by Merideth Harte & Jen Browning

www.sterlingpublishing.com/kids

Sign Language

by Lora Heller

STERLING CHILDREN'S BOOKS
New York

Imagine being able to tell your friend a secret from way across the playground. Or spelling something to your brother or sister that your parents don't understand. You can—with sign language!

The ABCs in sign language are called the Manual Alphabet, and using this alphabet to sign is called finger spelling. It's a fun way for you to chat with your friends or practice spelling any word you want.

Sign language is a great skill to have. You can practice finger spelling anywhere. It takes a little time and patience, but once you know how to do it you'll have your own secret language!

You can spell out the letters with the fingers of either hand, whichever one you feel most comfortable with. (The hand shown in the illustrations is the right hand.) For all of the letters except for G and H, your palm faces outward, toward the person you are talking to.

You're all set! Just open this book and learn your ABCs in American Sign Language. Then go out and spell anything and everything in your world!

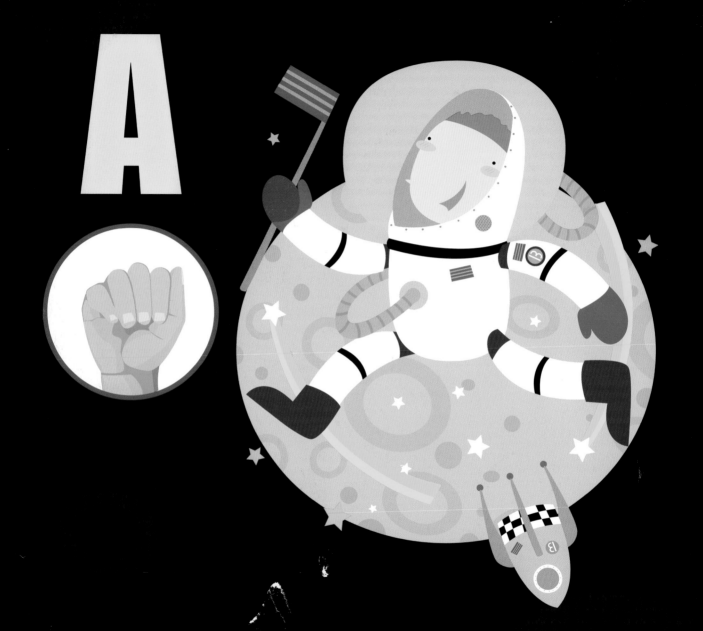

A

is for **astronaut**

B

is for **bird**

C

is for **crab**

D

is for **dragon**

E

is for **elephant**

F

is for **fish**

G

is for **giraffe**

H

is for **hippopotamus**

I

is for ice cream

J

is for **juggle**

K

is for **kangaroo**

L

is for **lion**

M

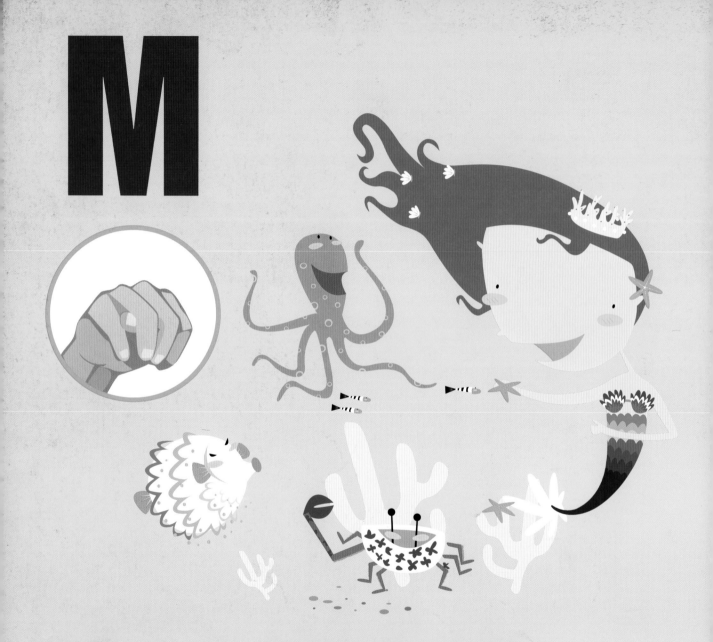

is for **mermaid**

N

Hoot...

is for **night**

O

is for **octopus**

P

is for **pirate**

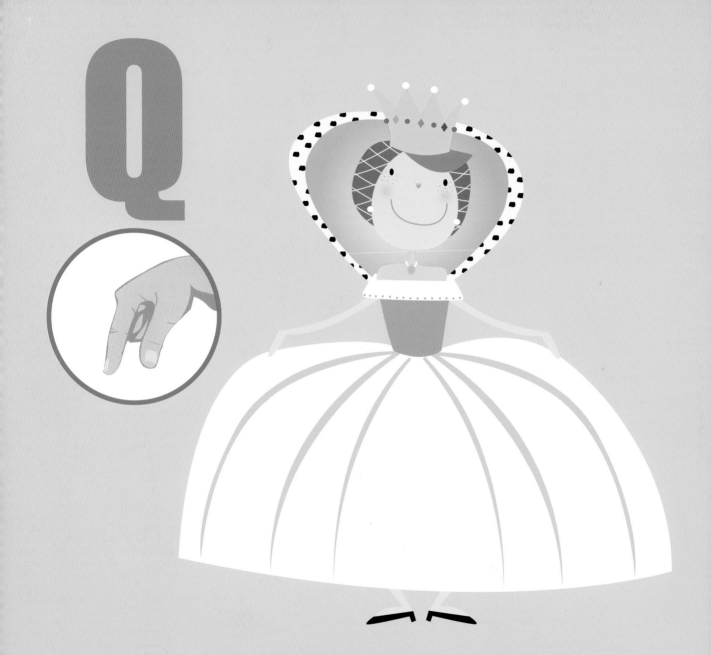

Q

is for **queen**

R

is for **robot**

S

is for **skiing**

T

is for **tiger**

U

is for **umbrella**

is for **vegetables**

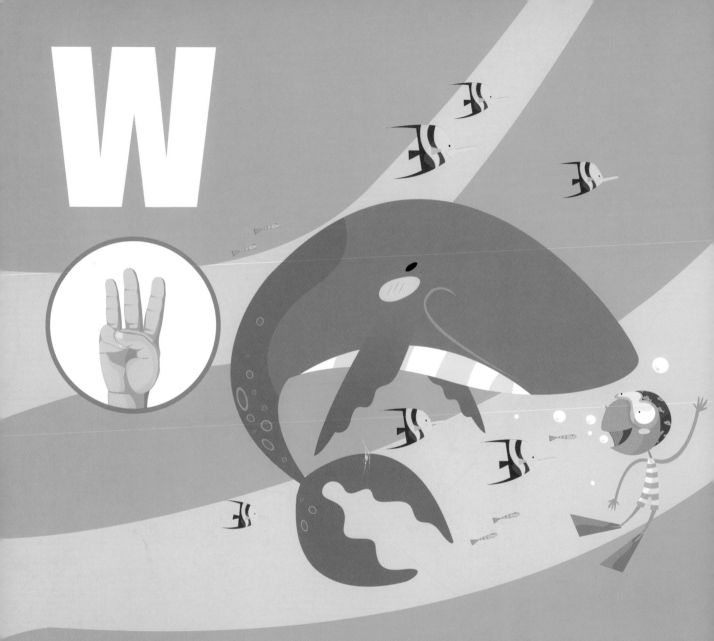

W

is for **whale**

is for **xylophone**

Y

is for yo-yo

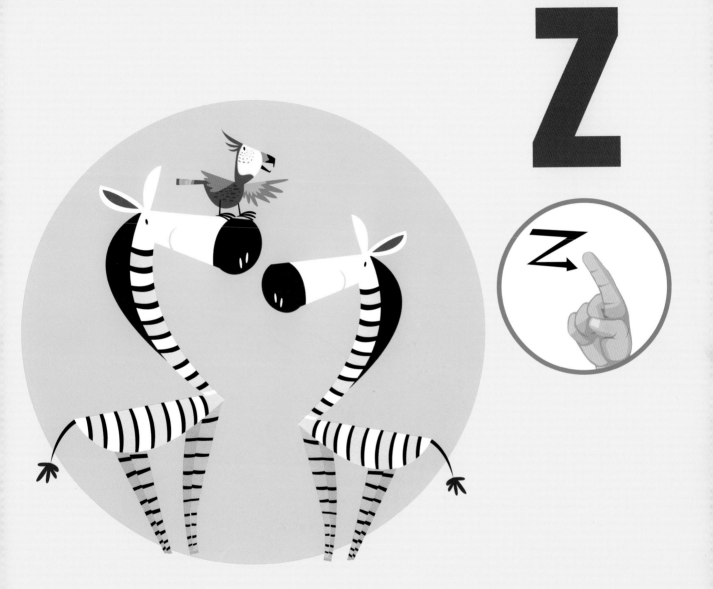

Z

is for **zebra**